# *Alabaster*
## Poems

*Marlaina Donato*

**Ekstasis Multimedia**
Blairstown, New Jersey

ALABASTER Copyright ©2012 Marlaina Donato All Rights Reserved. Printed in the United States of America. No part of this book may be used or reproduced in any way without written permission from the publisher except in the case of brief quotations embodied in articles and reviews.

Ekstasis Multimedia: www.booksandbrush.net

ISBN-13: 978-0615717913
ISBN-10: 0615717918

Photography and design: Marlaina Donato

*...for the winters of our lives*

*that teach us who we are...*

*Winterfires*

## Madonna

On this snow-hushed morning,

My four-year-old self is curled in sleep;

The room is smoke-tinged with burning oak.

She leans in to kiss me goodbye-

My mother in her amethyst coat with her alabaster face

Peering out from a halo of hooded fur.

Surely, she is an angel

Going out into a day deafened by white.

I fall back into dreams,

Knowing I will always remember her like this,

Madonna of the snows.

## Compensation

A waning winter moon

Spills her heart into the dawn…

Pausing in death, she silently waits in the trees.

Consumed by darkness, she has dreamt

Of this heartbeat, this sunrise

She could not have seen in her youth.

## Snowfire

The fire bleeds amber light;

Your hair smells like embers.

Lost in love's hour, we hadn't noticed the snow…

Now the steps are covered.

Lost in love's dreaming, we watch

The blowing white.

How am I to know

These moments, choreographed to your heartbeat,

Will be put away

Like leaves into a book of bitterness?

How am I to know

I will forget your hair in this light,

Its auburn scented with shadow?

That a forever from now,

On a morning haunted with ghosts,

I will open a book

And find the dead leaves of our season…

**New Skates**

Fresh snow patterned by new skates

A child and her father on the lake

When the years are collected

He will remember her green coat

With the silver buttons

And the plea, "Just one more minute?"

And she will remember him

Applauding an awkward turn

With pride in blue eyes bluer than heaven

## Tundra

Soul under snowdrifts

Footprints of the old self blown over

No light casting a shadow of the self that remains

Idle in the indifferent fist of circumstance

It is forgotten that for every December

There is an April

**Snow Angels**

The snow carves a cold blade into an onyx night;

We walk against the wind's diamond breath

Along the road lost hours ago.

I lean inside his corduroy

As we navigate the drifts in zigzag laughter.

"Do you remember our first winter?" he asks,

Folding me closer inside his coat

Until our footsteps tangle.

"Silent Night sung in French, blueberry

Pancakes in bed, and your black velvet jacket,"

I whisper memories.

We carve a road of remembrance

And wrestle in the white—

Long pause, a kiss.

His body burns over me,

And over his shoulder, parting clouds

And the glance of a single star.

## Circle

Alone, I take the old road.

The path is covered; leaves turn in their sleep.

December is an old woman,

And she passes me with gray eyes.

Where do they go, the hours we hold in vain?

Where do we go,

The selves that dissolve in dark water?

The heart is an old woman,

And she cries in the dusk.

The snows will cover us and the fires no one knew.

The forest will take us in

Without tears or regret.

New dreams will take root from the old;

Faith is an old woman, And she knows the way.

## Millennium

New Year's Eve, after twelve

Last year of the century, a toast on the beach

And a pause of laughter

Wondering

Who will cast resolutions

Upon a sea drunk with moonlight

And shake stars from their lover's hair

A hundred years from tonight

We will not see another last year of the century

So drink my kiss, my lover with stars in your hair

While the year is so fragile, so new

And so too this desire

## Inferno

A gold room, a pillow of thorns

Night deep in snow, soul on fire

This heart, a rose in a fist

Screaming to bloom

This hand pressed against the wall between us

Hour upon hour, year upon year,

Burning toward morning in vain

Praying for forgiveness and forgetfulness

## Pause

I memorized your smile

As we walked in the gold after the snow

With a white dog pulling five steps ahead.

You were beautiful with your dark fire against

Winter canvas,

So beautiful you hurt my eyes.

I memorized your gloved hand

As we walked in the gold after the snow,

And the trees threw a puzzle of shadows

Against our silence.

A white dog turned the corner;

We paused.

A lifetime later, we remain there, at the corner,

My heart on pause

In the shadows

Thrown by the words you never said.

## Winterscape

Moon pouring fire

Snow adorned with calligraphy of shadow

Night canvas

Violet brush stroke

Pastel morning

Wind and solitary cloud, a white smudge

By an unseen hand

## In a Library

The only ones here on this gray, uninspired morning,
On the third floor,
We nestle in books and conversation;
We taste each other's words… living embers
Amid sleeping volumes
Whose sires dream beneath the centuries.
You tell me that someday my pages
Will be collected here,
And I assure you that someday your fire
Will shake the world out of bed.
We plan.
We devise.
We aspire.
On an ashen morning
Pale with orphaned ambition,
We blaze in the arrogance of our youth.

# Gold Windows

## Winter Sunset

The west is a mural of light,

The east, a blue wash of silk;

The moon is a rising opal

As children color the street with fuchsia chalk,

Concrete canvas.

Church bells ring as day's light drowns

In a twilight starred with gold windows.

Children laugh on this last warm day before frost.

Joy without a reason.

## Slow Dance

Against your shoulder

In this shadow-scarred room

Against your chest

In this moon-pierced winter night

Against your belly

In this slow dance

Undress me with your thoughts

Run fingers of ideas along my spine

Do not touch me, just dream me

Dance me so close I no longer hear music

Only your exhale against my inhale

Let me forget myself

For minutes, hours, days

Against your sway

## Midnight

We linger over midnight coffee

As we taste each other's words for the first time;

The city's heart breaks in February cold.

For a moment, I forget

The child who sleeps in a doorway

And the sidewalks stained with slaughtered dreams;

For a moment, I forget

Someone else's eyes that once found me

In the neon nights

And the sounds from the streets

That echoed up to our room, our bed

Overlooking the park.

For a moment, I forget

The last time I was here…

We linger over midnight coffee,

Tasting each other's words,

Being in this city, again for the first time.

## Thaw

At dream's end, my fire will meet you,

Its heat no longer caged.

You will know

The hungers your eyes satiated,

The nights when I screamed your name into echo.

Only then, this deep river will rage from its ice

And all the words that dam my throat

Will mute even the song of God.

## A Saturday in December

We walked through the holiday village

With coats buttoned up and shawls over our hair;

We looked like children, cheeks flushed with smiles.

Winding fences were strung with lights

And snow fell in whisper, fine as mist.

We shared dreams over a pancake brunch

At the inn on the corner

(Not wishing for the berries served when in season.)

We were content, that winter day,

With friendship's pageantry.

## **Bitter Honey**

White door, stairs leading to an oval window
Stone hearth, old piano, bayberry candles
Entering through the old door
Expecting to find her, the girl I once was
Expecting her wide-eyed eagerness
And untouched soul
The willow chair, the yellow bedroom, the holly tree
All are here except the girl

Home for a spell, wars and lifetimes later
Home
So bitter, this honey
Scarred, this innocence
Soft, this wound of full circle

## Through the Eyes of Winter

Behind a pane of silence,

A winter-eyed man watches the world.

He knows well the mischief of the squirrel,

Joy of an April bird feeder,

The quiet wisdom of the deer.

His silence is born from knowing…

The answers to his own riddles of fate

And the trifling importance of the hourglass.

In the lined, celibate skin lies a map of experience,

Avenues of laughter, detours of uncertainty.

Passion still quakes in the tired heart,

Now with a quieter voice.

In the grandfather eyes, the boy still skips

With an undaunted smile.

Tired feet have not forgotten how to run,

And the drowsy mind still dreams.

Trodding through snowdrifts of limitation,

The winter-eyed remembers spring.

## January

A blue star hangs on the ear of twilight,

A heaven of heartbeats still to rise in an hour.

Westward moon, polished for her entrance,

Startles the darkness.

A silhouetted traveler pauses in step

And listens to the stars singing the night to birth.

## Transience

The first snow drapes the earth's naked symmetry;

Somewhere, day is lit beyond the sky's pewter veil.

Birds leave prints in the uninterrupted white

Like those who alight upon our lives

Until the winds blow over them.

What do we have from these visitations

To prove their existence?

The snow preserves a print for only so long.

Beauty alights like a bird

And then she is gone.

## Winter Amber

Red leaves entombed

In dark December ice

Autumn under glass

## Rain

Through a long tunnel of days, finally, your voice

Our worlds touch

And I bear the weight of heaven

I love you, as the rain closes us in

I press your words against the storm

I love you, no need to choke on the unspoken

You already know

## Yeats

You are a miracle, in your open white shirt
You and your hands more gentle than a verse of Yeats
You and your fingers pale and bronzed in this light
As the fire spends its wealth

We are a miracle, together on this winter night
A small universe sparking in the dark
My touch inside your open white shirt
More gentle than a verse of Yeats

*Snowblind*

## November

November trees, skeletons of the year
I am here, a question unanswered
Past the point of sound, a syllable of silence
I have no language but a song unwritten

Street lights pierce the windshield
Left turn home to nowhere
Shout at the gods for someone to hold
Anyone
The man with the silver ring
The woman with summer eyes
Anything
A handful of dust
A pocket of light
Anywhere
The dirt road
The over-grown garden
The grave beneath 300 miles left behind

## White

A slant of light on a white piano

Pale, beautiful fingers

Long and lyrical

Dancing over white keys

Pale, beautiful, loyal and living

Beneath the player's persuasion

No gold of sun, no petals of spring

White morning

White hands

White keys

A pause of white

## New Year's Dawn

The winter dawn is a cup of gold;
Timidly, cautiously, the soul takes a sip.

A memory dances in the light…
Broken wings remember the flight;
A memory dances in the light.

Morning shimmers with gold, soon to die into silver;
For a dream, the earth is young,
So young, a shadow could break its heart.

## The Bridge

I see her standing on the bridge

During a morning snow.

She does not offer a word;

Our eyes brush,

Joy's poverty in her glance.

I smile…

*This morning is broken-winged,*

*But there will be a day of rejoicing,*

*Dear sparrow in the snow,*

*A day of rejoicing.*

## Preservation

I watch you read in front of the window
Halo of hair, pale-painted mouth
Blue tumble of sleeve
All silver-lined in virgin winter light
Quick flight of thought and wire-rimmed glasses
Answering the sun in reflection
Artist's hands and the gentle turning of the page
The lifting of rain-blue eyes for a pause of smile
You are more than a man—half fire, half shadow
For a breath, you are the morning's canvas
Forever preserved in the memory
Of a woman who loved you

## Window

In cold pre-dawn fire

A star burns in the East

A candle in some distant window

## **Inaudible**

Veined leaf, once green summer on your cheek

Now blood-stained russet

The sun burns toward winter

Leaf-heart, slowly starving for light

Knowing the certain end, the anemic fall into the wind

Screaming in colors translated as joy

While the inaudible rages beneath your gold

And the sun burns—heedless, deaf, and fat on eternity

## Avalanche

Old woman, time-ravaged skin

Clinging to the bone

Hair a white wisp

She waits in the hallway

In a graveyard for the living

As they change the soiled sheets

And talk in Spanish

Old woman with eyes like mine

Who once drank wine under the stars

And laughed when she got caught in the rain

And loved someone she can no longer remember

An old woman pleading to go home

As I pass her on my way out

Old woman with eyes like mine

**Alabaster**

Winter night chiseled from alabaster

The day unraveled, your body undressed

Hunger unfurled on white linen

## Elegy

Autumn doe beside the road

Curled in graceful death

Once beating heart now mute

Beneath wind-weighted grasses

Forests will remember you

And the hills that wore your tracks in December

Coat turned silver for the snows

Cast off like a tired dream

While your soul nestles somewhere in summer

Somewhere far from this highway grave

Sleep

Beautiful dancer

Sleep

## Spent

I came to you late in the season

When you were burdened with years

And your flowers and fruit had seen their hour-

I came to know only thorns,

Unaware that beneath your snows

A beautiful summer had once been there.

## Winter-Speak

Encased in ice, I have learned to speak winter.

Sentenced to snow, I have surrendered to cold chastity.

But in the heart of this tundra,

Behind stone that cannot burn,

A fire rages in your colors.

Resigned to paralysis, I have married stillness,

But in the isolation of nights,

Behind stone that cannot move,

I dance barefoot to your summer.

Buried in white sleep, I accept the sterile harvest,

But in the wasteland of want,

Behind stone that cannot hunger,

I ravage your orchards.

Enshrouded in futility, I inherit compromise,

But in this prison of silence

Behind stone that cannot speak,

I sing

I sing this love.

*North Wind*

## Manna

Pages yellowed by time
Stark words etched in ember
A signature—a pirouette in ink, right hand corner
Her name untouched, her spirit long flown
No longer the name of my mother
But the name of a woman who spun words
Blood-stained words of light
A woman
A glorious sun burning in verse
A forgotten poet singing to her daughter
Who holds her words like bread
In a time of famine
Bread of dark sustenance
Of grain that says, "I too hungered."
Bread for these dark nights
And dawns with no answers

## Ending

Dry fields are bleached by winter's breath,

Dry fields raped by time

And corn bending in death.

I stand at the rim of the world

As night comes in on fire,

Broken shards of ember over harvest waste.

I stand at the rim of the world

And watch you die in the sun.

The universe seeps through

The hole gutted in the center of me;

The ground is a river where you bleed out of me.

Dawn will rise; spring will dance;

These fields will again know lover's green.

I stand at the rim of the world

Knowing your heart has no return.

The sky turns toward ash and sleep,

And I own nothing, nothing

But the wind blowing through where you used to be.

## Price

The sun retreats, igniting long-dead leaves

In amber resurrection before the first fist of snow.

The sun retreats, spilling eons of solitude traveled.

*Who or what do you look to when you too need light?*

Who waits with lantern in hand

For those who make their own light?

## Exit

Winter's final snow bonnets the world…
Crimson buds shiver in dreaming
And the white-gowned hydrangea is a lady in lace.
With the season's closing, you leave my life
As you entered it, during the last snow
Before spring's first whisper.
I will continue onward and with each milestone,
Pause to remember our laughter;
With each year's closing snow,
I will see the hydrangea wear her lace
As my heart, cold and proud,
Wears the beauty of your memory.

## Snowrose

My footprints make a pathway to your grave;

Sounds of the city trespass the heavy iron gates.

How thin the thread

Between worlds, realized only now

As my boots violate the chaste night snow.

The first snow remains on granite

But has vanished from the soil

Covering your memory.


I leave you a crimson flower

As a nearby angel watches

And dons winter's first white on her wings.

**Venus**

Venus is a burnt opal

In the corner of sky above the church;

On a night like this, long ago,

Our laughter punctured the darkness

While the world slept

And Lady Guadalupe smiled.

Far, how far it is since

That cold street charred with piñon,

That mural of starlight,

And the plans and dreams spilling from plenty.

It is familiar, this penance of bliss,

Its thorn through my soul

And the sound of church bells;

It is familiar, this prayer,

Pressed like a burnt opal to my chest

And its unanswered futility.

## Ritual

A lone bird drifts in the wind,

Painting silhouetted freedom

Against a pewter sky.

Others gather, and in the pale smoky light,

One, two, three…still more,

Circling above fallen, bloodless leaves,

Soaring in ritual,

Death dance.

## Memory Keeper

Snow-crust and the dialogue of our boots
Along cobblestone
Bells from the old church and your breath
Against my hair
I will not forget these things
Or the color of your scarf like crushed sapphire
I will not forget my hand in your back pocket
As you tell me the history of this city
And where to find the best croissants
Will you remember this when we are old…
Remember holding me against the wind
And how fragile, how indestructible
You have made me?
I will not forget these things
Or the color of crushed sapphire
As you hold me against the wind

## Sea Glass

Winter sea of broken glass

Crushed beneath the weight of gray

Inside, wrapped in the summer of your arms

You feed me with marmalade fingers

Laughter over a late breakfast

Tea amber in the cup

Blue eyes faceted with light

Contentment

## Threshold

Heaven's heart weeping white

Trees in royal slumber

We stand in the threshold

Longing to fly into the night

To walk until dawn

Newness too beautiful to scar with boot prints

Pristine pause of time

It is enough, this threshold

And heaven's heart weeping white

## Morning Walk

Your body is a moving prayer

In this brightness, holy hour

Of light and lover's arms breaking the winds

Arms strong as the distant mountains

Imposing in violet

Beyond the crushed petals of water's edge

Kiss, an epiphany of warm oblivion

In this brightness, holy hour

Love making all things new

## 70 Degrees

Winter quit his job today

And spring dusted off her dancing shoes

The sun came back a hero

And left his autograph across the hills

The winds reveled in the heavens

And birds gossiped about winter's breach of contract

Leaves played tag across the lawn

And every tired heart remembered

What it is like to be in love

## Winter

Embraced by the North's infertile breath,

Winter arrives with yew braided in her hair.

Barren, she is akin to Death,

'Tis poison fruit her sable tresses bear.

Look for her eyes in the blue of a December twilight

And quietly listen for her trailing gowns.

When the moon wears a halo of whispered white

'Tis then she empties her purse of frosted down.

She bejewels the trees when the year is new

And buffs the lake for sharpened silver blades.

Morning sun ignites her prism's hue,

'Tis why we forgive her heart of spades.

## Marlaina Donato

Poetry is the golden child of observation and catharsis- or so it is for poet-author-artist Marlaina Donato.

Her passion for words was sparked at age ten when her mother gave her a copy of Whitman's *Leaves of Grass*. Marlaina soon found her own Muse, scribbling onto bits of paper and in journals. Reading and writing poetry became necessity- bread for the soul and a compass to live by.

Marlaina lives in rural New Jersey with her husband Joe and their canine muse Noah.

Contact: Ekstasis Multimedia, LLC at www.booksandbrush.net

www.ingramcontent.com/pod-product-compliance
Lightning Source LLC
Chambersburg PA
CBHW061257040426

42444CB00010B/2407